CONTENTS

For George Hogg and Phill King

Moonshot

That night, everybody stayed up late
To watch the moon landing
Whilst I, almost weightless, knowing
Not to scratch at my chickenpox,
Orbited a sleepless planet
With moonshot eyes, buoyed
By low voices, murmurs downstairs,
A faint cheer as the Eagle landed.
Then, in the silence that followed,
A tug of fear: What if I'm stranded?

On my bedside table, a polar bear
Perched on a glacier mint,
A giraffe dipped to the watering hole,
Its neck a see-saw yard of ale.
I knew nothing of its workings then:
How a rising thread of alcohol
Tips the head, cools and contracts
At the taste of water, a sip, a shiver,
Back to the bulb at the base of the neck,
An unslaked thirst, unshakeable fever.

Returning, I know why astronauts
Turn to drink or God with visions
Of Earth as small as a marble,
Rolled blue-glass, milky swirls.
And now that polar bears float south
On shrinking floes in vodka seas
And parched giraffes burst into flames
And the skies stream with stripes and stars,
The man in the moon's smooth blank screen
Mirrors a face of craters and scars.

Watching Over

I hover in the doorway
watching you sleep
– above the covers
your face half shows –
a breath, a whisper
let no demon come
between the floorboards
and my toes.

Strawberry Field

Smoothing the waxed paper
Of a Fruit Bonbon,
A red one,
She recoils, the small
Ghost of a cry escapes her:
Total recall.

A girl of nine rises
Early and strips the bed.
Never a word
Of this. Dead to the world
On tranquillisers,
Her mother has heard

Nothing. She goes at dawn,
A bundle in her arms,
Through the farmyard
And Pick Your Own fields,
Towards a far corner
Where the yield

Is low and fruit left to rot,
The air sickly sweet.
And there (not wedding-
But winding-sheet) she buries
White cotton, spotted
With strawberries.

Swimming Clear

My goggles would fill with water. I'd
Manage a length and a half of breast-
Stroke (slowest of the Slow, mortified)
Put my foot down and wade the rest.
Meanwhile, caulked with Vaseline,
She'd be ploughing a lonely furrow
Over and over in the Fast Lane.
A pool with no end, deep or shallow.

She said she was always seen as weird.
On the first-leg of the relay
At the Inter-School Gala, cheered
As she built up a lead, she couldn't rely
On her team-mates, tumble-turned, kept on
Through screams of blue murder from all sides,
Swam all four lengths, four strokes, and *won* –
Climbed out to silence, disqualified.

Rising to the scare-story bait
She dared to swim Cogenhoe Lake.
A drowned man. A girl in a boat,
Three trailing fingers lost to a pike.
She sized it up in lengths of the pool
– No sweat – but felt a touch of cold
In the heated lanes, training before school
That winter, the brush of a limb, green-gold.

I emerge into the blur of the sun,
Red-eyed, blinking. She could never
Quite rinse the chlorine from her skin.
Back in our first days together
I dreamt of a glacial mountain lake
Braced for the hypothermic shock:
She takes the plunge. The clarity of loss
As I watch her, naked, make it across.

Sea Shantih

Wide-eyed anemones
Sway in the underwater breeze.

Tiny fish, open lips,
Rise consensually from the depths.

Transported in a glass-hulled boat,
Partners-in-crime, we slowly float

All the way to Botany Bay.
Heave away, haul away.

Shantih – peace (Sanskrit)

11

The Effect of Coastal Processes on the Beach at Amroth

We blew into our hands for warmth,
With calipers and a hypothesis
Measuring the size and roundedness
Of pebbles, the effect of coastal processes.
The set of results confounded us.
Maybe there'd been a recent storm:

The size of pebbles did *not* diminish
In the direction of longshore drift,
Not according to our sample.
There must've been a shift
In the prevailing wind. It's simple,
He explained to his girlfriend, we're in this

Together – she was eight days late –
But as they sat at the high tide
Mark, watching the swash and backwash,
Waves of attrition, a multitude
Of tiny cuffing knocks, the fact was
That in the fading daylight

Hushed and rocked she'd reached a decision,
Calm, before a sea of troubles.
In my palm's a small flat stone:
The flints we skim return as pebbles.
Of the beach at Amroth's population
Would anyone ever miss this one?

A Diver in the Waiting Room

Staring into the aquarium
I'm alright, Jacques,
Safe from the bends or shark attack
And relieved I never did become
What I said I wanted to as a boy.
My fixation: a toy

Diver on the gravel bed,
Clumpy boots,
Pumped-up thick-skinned suit,
Helmet clamped over his head,
His breath an opalescent sigh
Rising to a sky

Of unstormy tropical blue.
The smaller, quicker
Fish, bright nerves, flicker
And dart in and out of view.
They've plants, rocks, every wish.
The largest fish,

At four inches a barracuda,
Slowly wanders
Over to the diver, ponders
Some microscopic specks of food
About his person. A brush of lips
And over he tips.

I'd already put aside
Childish things
– Stabilisers, water wings –
When one of Cousteau's divers died,
My favourite for his killer looks
And the risks he took,

Stabbed in a bar-room brawl.
I couldn't stand
The obvious irony: on dry land.
Hearing the receptionist call
I come up for air at long last
Too fast, too fast.

A Jar of Rhyme

A jar of ale for a drowning man
The room begins to swim
I came in like Desperate Dan
Leave as Gentleman Jim.

O hush, man, don't shout
You'll wake the baby in the manger
Whose father was always in doubt
And mother was even stranger.

And now we must endeavour
To go our separate ways
Think well of me whatever
The Mail on Sunday says.

Rudderless as a Manx cat
I'll make my way home alright,
Scuffing the WELCOME mat
Before the stiffest test of the night:

Though I climb with tiptoe grace,
A dainty ballerina,
Towards the summit the staircase
Plays up like a concertina.

Cavalry Miniatures

i 'This always happens'
after Goya

Fatalism:
the cavalry charge,
the fall
of a horse

foetal,
its dying face
the face of
a foal.

ii A Horseman of Thessaly

There was nothing to explain
His arrival in the warzone,
And we buried the remains
Separately of course:
The man's naked torso,
His headless horse.

But the girl who heard him canter
From the distant past –
Then a gap –
Then the sound of the blast,
Always held that a centaur
Died in her lap.

iii *Panic Attack*

I'd never been on a horse before
Mounting Panic,
Which threw me completely.

How I ever, as a boy
– The rows and rows of stoic soldiers
Lined up so neatly –

Led the charge of the dragoons
To that famous victory
Utterly defeats me.

iv *Cavalry Officers*

Bright and rigid, riding tall,
A group of four
Horsemen on my bedroom wall,
Groomed for war.

A birthday gift, but I was bored
Of playing soldiers:
They grew more miniature
As I grew older.

One day (*Make Love, Not War!*)
I saw them for what they were,
Replaced them with a poster
Of the Fab Four.

But now, all slogans grown cryptic,
I rein in my fear
As, inexplicably apocalyptic,
They reappear.

v Virgin Soldier

As he wanders the woods of delirium
The infantryman who stood his ground
Before a line of chargers, looming
Large, a rumble of hooves, the horses
Of love and war – joined forces –
Plunging and rising, nostrils fuming,
Astounded at his own heart's sound
The maid he bleeds for enters a clearing
Leading a milky unicorn
Chastely by its red-tipped horn.

vi Heat and Thrust

Just this, from the crusades –

how the hefty stallions of Christendom
had a tendency, in the flaring heat
and thrust of battle, to rear,

to throw their riders, less out of fear
than the desire to mount
and slake the thirst

of a sleek and flaming Barbary mare.

Two Swords

Richard

An iron bar propped between two rocks.
A broadsword, imperiously tempered,
Raised above the crown of the head.
Arms numbed by the cleaving shock.

Saladin

A square of silk thrown into the air
Left to drift back down across a scimitar
So imperturbable, slender and blue
As to pare the scarf delicately in two.

Cock-crow at The Eastgate

Morning paper and milk in hand,
I pass my dive of a local with its tang of the jakes
As the cockerel in the backyard defiantly takes,
At the gates of the east, one last stand.

The pub's condemned. On its sign
A figure emerges from an arch, peeling and shabby,
Leaving the faded spires of Reading Abbey
At the hour of lauds. Mumbling lines

Of faint praise, he gravitates
Through dissolute red-brick streets, darkly cowled, down
To the Thames, to stand illuminated on Broken Brow,
Awaiting the henchmen of Henry VIII.

The end of the world as we know it.
A sullied *lully lullay*, an ashen bloodshot sunrise,
The strangled notes – hung-over, lovesick, unwise –
As Chanticleer clears his throat.

In the Moslem-owned corner-shop
They know of a Day on which the celestial
Cock fails to crow. All of us, ascetic and bestial,
Falling silent (the spoon stops

Above the bowl) for we must die.
Wake up! On the front-page the Middle East's in flames,
On the Corn Flakes packet a bird stakes its claim:
A strangely awry triumphal cry.

Kennet Mouth

Tonight a pair of swans, heads tucked back,
Pillowed on white, float a long eddying swell
Of oblivion, black as a river of Hell.

Here, where the Kennet meets the Thames,
A river of forgetting meets a river
Of regret, Lethe meets Acheron,

An announcement I can't quite follow
Carries downstream from Reading Station
– Is this the train you're leaving on?

*

Slowly it approaches, old rolling stock,
The last train all but empty of souls,
Sparking the sky above Brunel's bridge

Beneath which, one Halloween, the Pandemonium
Marching Band (sax, tuba, accordion, drum)
Struck up a spirited dirge, struck up

A spectral replica on the other side,
Echoing to Kingdom Come in the damp arch
As torches threw shadows on the far wall.

I followed, wheeling the accordionist's bike
– The cycle path strewn with broken glass –
Past Blake's Lock and The Jolly Anglers,

The gas monitor's persistent hiss,
The lifebelt holder with its stump of rope,
The scrap of grass where we turned and kissed,

Things still in place, the things we list
To stem the haemorrhage of memories,
Words that were spoken, light on a face.

*

Issuing from the throat of the bridge,
The Kennet, brimming with volume, mouths
The same slow vow, letting go,

As it did before – the same *I do* –
Giving itself up to a greater flow
Whilst I, knowing myself undone,

Knowing it's time to go, hold back
On the brink of a cold consummation,
The clank of the train dwindling to London.

The Melodians

Who originally sang By the Rivers of Babylon?
Was the tiebreak question in the pub quiz
That led to his rant, fired by injustice.
He stormed to the front – *It was the Melodians!* –

But no-one had heard of the old reggae band;
His friends shrugged; the girl he'd asked along
Looked away; and so, in the right but in the wrong,
He left them queuing for a damp basement club, stranded

In a strange land, by ancient fluorescent waters,
The Thames doubling as the Euphrates, hanging baskets
Dripping from every pub, taking himself to task,
Full of desire and dread for its delirious daughters

Hopelessly carried away and only becoming calm
At the weeping of the willows, Rastafarian trees,
Remembering – out of humiliation, humility –
The sweet voices of the slaves.
                              A vengeful psalm.

The Only Shoes

They're the only shoes I'd commit suicide in
She laughs, leaning into her friend,
Tripping the hardcore light fantastic:

High-heel sling-backs, spangly red plastic,
Imelda Marcos wouldn't be seen dead in.
They'll be history when the music ends

Ankle-straps broken, hobbled, raw,
Alongside the pumps gaping with holes
From a 1930s speakeasy danceathon

Poor girls' dreams, shoes to die for
Like Emma Bovary's pink satin mules,
Cleopatra's sandals, snakeskin toe-thong.

Over the Menai Strait

Here's me at twenty – seen as if from above –
Crossing the bridge over the Menai Strait
      With Stephanie,
Sleet needling, gusted in at gale-force 8,
Cursing us in our fingerless gloves,
      A numb epiphany

As we laugh and grope for the icy railing.
No high-wire feat, but one of hope
      And apprehension:
Shrieking metal, the road turned skipping-rope,
Buckling at the knees, thick cables flailing.
      A faltering suspension

Of disbelief. We'd skipped the afternoon session
Of the University Nightline Conference.
      That morning, some matey
Evangelist cornered me, breathing nonsense
About Self-Interest-As-Altruism,
      Pure 1980s.

But what if he had a point after all?
Of course the thing is to be there for others.
      But what if, when the phone
Rings – you jump, a deep breath to recover –
Lifting the receiver to that last-ditch call
      Someone voices your own

Thoughts? A memory from the Wild Woods:
Two boys trying to keep the string taut
      Across a wide pond
Between margarine-tubs. A hollow and fraught
Can you hear me? An SOS from childhood
      To which no-one responds.

Fifteen years on and I'm still trying
To make that crossing, keep on my toes
    Over an angry sea,
The bridge easing from its supple throes,
A gull more flung by the wind than flying
    To Anglesey.

Lore or Mess

All the teachers were marking bad,
All the poets botching words.
 Who to blame? Dummy and maddy.

A milky-smooth Sinister of the Crown
Was found, got with his own shun:
 Howling, the press punted in hacks.

Fights broke out, Rods v Mockers,
Pairs of lovebirds killing and booing.
 TV chefs added mist to the grill.

Wired and teary doctors and nurses
Treated soldiers, deft for lead.
 Outside, at dusk, the bogs darked.

Three Late Landscapes by Poussin

His eye was not dim, nor his natural force abated
Deuteronomy, 34.7

I   In *Blind Orion Searching for the Rising Sun*
                              after the nights
     stumbling over roots and moss-grown boulders
                              with clouded sight
     the giant strides – a guide balanced on his shoulder –
                              towards the truth,
     an eye-opening dawn, a salve for what was done
                              in the blindness of youth,
     the rush of spring, moving through the world anew,
                              green primal form,
     the stumps of torn trees, a lush thick dew,
                              remembered storms.

II   It's not the storms, apocalyptic, that transfix me,
                              bring me to dream,
     but the *Landscape with a Calm*, when, mid-afternoon,
                              everything seems
     to lean with the goatherd on his stick, late June,
                              and even the horse
     that bolts from the scene, jolting us from fixity,
                              holds still of course,
     all part of a preternatural idyll, an artistic spell
                              of clearer-than-ever
     – the turquoise lake and quietly reflective citadel –
                              unchanging weather.

III With *The Spies Returning from the Promised Land*
                                as shadows lengthen
towards evening, harvesting the autumn gold,
                                desire strengthens
for a last bacchanal before the year turns cold,
                                a feast of stolen
apples, pomegranates, figs too big for the hand,
                                sweet, swollen,
the holiest fruit, each purple eucharistic grape
                                the size of a plum,
plucked by all who face this landscape, agape
                                at the life to come.

Refusenik

Those stories of virgin brides
Bathing in streams of milk,
Of whores, almond-eyed,
Purses of honey and silk.

We clamoured for a taste
– Manna from the sky –
Wiped the juice from our chins
And fed on every lie.

*

And so it came to pass
From Joshua to Sharon
From Jericho to Jenin
The holy trumpets blown

The tanks rolling in
Under a hail of stones.
None was spared but Rahab
For the kindness she had shown.

*

Her sons, walking bombs,
Bulldozers at first light,
A dawn of milk and honey
Over the Golan Heights

(Milk of an onion, honey from wasps)
The hills blue and mauve.
A woman wails and spits
In the bitter orange grove.

Amanuensis

At first I tried to write down everything,
Amanuensis to a blind God,
To keep up with His runaway train of thought,
The huge conceptual leaps, chain lightning,
Winds of genesis moving over the waters
Foweles in the frith, fisses in the flod.

It gave me writer's cramp. At last He stopped
To consider. And I saw what He couldn't see:
An inquisitor had come to my windowsill,
A clockwork blackbird that flickered and hopped
Before a backdrop of showy frills,
The slow can-can of the cherry trees.

I started up again with some reluctance.
His insights seemed more humdrum
And soon I was lagging far behind.
He slowed right down, gave me a chance
To catch up – or was He too flagging, mind
Grinding to a halt, some knotty conundrum

Knitting His brow, strangling language? I squirmed
In my seat, put down my pen in defiance
Of the Word. (It hurt, I could tell).
The blackbird had been answered with a worm,
The wind had got up and as some blossom fell
I followed its drift, a scribe to silence.

Matted Grass

We wade more than walk
Into the long grass
Of old flames
And simmering shame,
The parted stalks
Closing behind us.

Up to our waists
In Queen Anne's Lace,
Skirting thistles
– Purple-crowned
Barbaric majesties
Of this common ground –

Moving like thieves
Without words
We drop from the sight
Of all but the birds
And bees, to part
With our fig-leaves

On the matted grass.
When a small plane passes,
Its monotone buzz
Obliging me to say
Someone is watching us,
You brush it away.

Gloucestershire

I remember a thump,
the swelling of a bruise,
the brown mulch
in the wax of the green,
the maggot-holes
and globules of mould,
the butting and nuzzling
of cidery wasps,
their last dazed gasps

toppling into that vat
that barrel
that Falstaff of an apple.

Bob Witherspoon's Cherries

He goes back up the rungs
    To a favourite pastime,
Another year younger,
    As ever, than last time.

And as his fingers reach
    Towards a bumper crop
The sound of giggles and shrieks
    Breezes through the tree-tops.

Their breathless laughter dies.
    Hands shoot from the leaves
To rob him of his prize.
    Oho! He rolls his sleeves

To play it out with them,
    The slips of girls he'd pip
To a slender wishbone stem.
    But when the tree is stripped

What cherries have I won?
    I'm no match for a maiden.
And though I've had my fun
    I go back down unladen.

The Ass

At dusk – it must've been about midsummer –
Stealing to and from the nearest copse
On Foxhill, listening to an owl's rumour,
We dug up enough of the rich topsoil

To cover his carpet two inches deep.
We lined walls with rhododendron, placed holly
In the window, laced the ceiling with creepers,
Strewing his mattress with flowers
To complete our folly.

Earlier, we'd used all of our puckish powers
Persuading Lorna Brampton to stay awake
And lie like Titania in her bower.
Now we waited to see what an ass he would make.

And when he returned, clearly in need of bed,
Opened the door and saw where she lay,
Sure enough, the long ears sprang from his head.
We threw back our necks and started to bray.

The Sacrifice of the Ass

A young ass is slain in honour of the stiff guardian
of the countryside: the curse is shameful but beseems the god
Ovid, *Fasti*

One drowsy day, Silenus
– Hot, itchy, slumped and sore,
Trundling along on his ass,
Massively bored –

Was alerted by a sudden
Pricking up of mangy ears.
Always a reliable sign
Some wayside flower was near.

And sure enough, there she lay,
The wood-nymph, Lotis,
Asleep in the shade.
And then, tingling, he noticed

His goatish master, red-faced
Priapus, creeping up
On the unattended maid,
Unable to believe his luck:

So elusive a beauty
Unguarded by deities!
Silenus stopped to watch,
Whilst, bothered by flies,

The ears of his donkey flinched.
The god inched forward, tentatively,
Scarcely able to contain himself.
But just as he met her lovely

Perfume, just as he entered
The cool of the shade,
Just as he reached to clasp her girdle,
Silenus' saddle-ass brayed.

And that, petal, is why we must
Make this sacrifice today.
I know, I'm sorry –
The ass you've fed such honeyed hay.

Barabbas

The Nazarene? Yes, he showed his face
At some of the early resistance meetings.
He never said much, didn't start bleating
When things got ugly, but he once put the case
    For *revolution without bloodshed* – then went
    Scouring the desert for enlightenment.

So I thought they were stringing me along,
The smirking turnkeys who brought *good news*
Saying I'd to thank the *King of the Jews*,
Doing a condemned man one last wrong.
    My brothers, a nest of vipers to the last,
    Called me *scab* and spat as I passed.

I lashed out. One gaoler grabbed me by the hair.
Another kicked and punched me and said
I was a dog who should by rights be dead.
They hauled me over to the foot of the stairs.
    It was then that I caught wind of the crowd,
    Growing, with each step, increasingly loud

Barabbas! Give us Barabbas! baying
For my blood, I thought. My own people!
All the fight went out of me... I crumpled
When the palace guards came wading in, laying
    Into me, dragged me on my knees to stand
    Before Pilate. He was drying his hands.

Forgive me, he said, *a last taste of violence*
Before your reprieve. He seemed agitated,
Pacing up and down, deliberating.
And then the crowd outside fell silent.
   He stopped before me – *Are rebels grown meek?* –
   And raised his hand as if to slap my cheek

But he gestured instead to the balcony.
As I staggered out, an almighty cheer
Rose to greet me. Then a voice at my ear
Holy men backed by Roman money
   Made me turn around, brought me face to face
   With the donkey due to die in my place.

Alexamenos graffito, Rome 2nd century

Pygmalion

Having dealt blows
and gouged,
taken things out
on you (at pains
neither to stun
nor bruise your stone)
scooped the cwm
of a collarbone,
flat-chiselled
long contours,
scrubbed you down
with abrasives,
I'll rub polish in,
emollient,
soothing your skin.

Tithonus

Waking first thing, he saw her
Pallid in a pink cagoule
And sky-blue skirt, public school:
Not Dawn then, but Aurora.

As she came through the park
The winter gloom began to lift,
As if she might revoke her gift.
And so he lurched from the dark

Rhododendron in which *uncouthe
Unkiste* he'd spent the night,
To fall, an absolute fright,
At the foot of eternal youth.

She screamed. His straggly beard,
Blackened piss-lacquered coat,
Her name like gravel in his throat.
The blinding rays as she disappeared.

Alcmena

I knew he wouldn't die,
My blue-faced son,
Half-drowned, half-choked,
Twelve labours in one:

He was holding up the sky
When my waters broke.

Tutankhamen

I   I was dismayed by the death-mask:
It didn't match the huge plastic
Replicas they were touting outside
(Someone said a *boy*-king had died).
We'd queued for an hour in the drizzle
To shuffle, reverential and miserable,
Through artefacts and standing tombs,
The hushed air of the Egypt Room.

But what happens next can't be right.
Everything recedes into night.
My parents? Sister? I can't see them.
There's no-one left in the museum
As I linger for a moment longer
Than I mean to, press my fingers
Red-tipped against the radiant case,
Transfixed by his rapt gold face.

II   What, in that moment, did I know?
Nothing of power failures in Cairo
The very instant the seals were broken,
The tales of lethal spores awoken,
The Earl of Carnarvon's favourite dog
Howling at home like the jackal-god,
Anubis, as he followed and patrolled
The last journey of his master's soul.

And nothing of the faith in Pharaoh
Climbing a tetrahedral stairway
To reach the apex of time and space,
Enter the stars and resume his face.
No, I only knew as I met
Those prized eyes of blue and jet,
Those eyes that never flinch or close,
That nothing could ever disturb this repose.

The Elgin Marbles Dispute

for Nikos Pyromalis

Let's settle it with a game of *tavli*
in a quiet taverna,
just the clack clack
of stacked counters
and the skittery roll of dice
carved deep
from the anklebones
of a Peloponnesian sheep.

Lines for a Letter Carver

for Pip Hall

Stone has its own scent
– A crushed together store
Of weathers – lifting the moment
Your chisel splits the ore.

Stone has its own light
(All through the dark it waits)
Words coming up white
On matt black slate.

Stone has its own song
Too deep to hear, a strain
A pulse you follow along
Milky marble veins.

Without a trace of violence
The point is driven home.
You tap into the silence
Of riven green stone.

Black Light

sometimes something
in black & white
momentarily
catches the light

the molten keys
of Coltrane's sax
jewelled throat
of Maria Callas

the film flares
black – we stare
dazzled by the
dark, the glare

Home Planet

Our nearest yellow-crayoned star
Blazes on the freezer door,
Central to the solar system.
As we begin a whistle-stop tour
Of the planets, I'm asked to list them:
Mercury, Venus, Earth, Mars

Each is blu-tacked in its place.
His mother helped him measure
The distances inbetween to scale.
He takes a proprietorial pleasure
As I name them, follow his trail
Into an immensity of space:

Jupiter's on the nearest wall;
The washing-machine's where we visit
Saturn; over by the light switch
Neptune floats (or is it
Uranus? I can never think which);
About halfway down the hall

I find whichever one it's not,
Felt-tipped, a scribbled blue;
Lastly, I manage to discover
Pluto in the downstairs loo,
Fallen from its spot above the
Radiator – much too hot

For such a far-flung icebound orb.
We stick it back up. My tour's
Complete. He's tall enough now
To open the frosted-glass front door.
As he reaches up to show me how,
A shadow looms, the doorbell

Goes, and suddenly he's thrown,
Hurrying back to his mum.
It's left to me. I welcome someone
Numb with cold in the winter sun,
Another guest light years from home,
That 'planet not unlike our own'.

Gargoyle

The wind must have changed
And my face got stuck,
Scrunched up, deranged,
Permanently thunderstruck

Under the spire's tapering
Prayer, eight numb
Centuries, a gurning leering
Urchin – sore thumb –

Little Jack Horner,
One of four brothers
Banished to the corners
Of the eyes of each other,

Buggered, mouths washed out.
A filthy storm's brewing,
Bruising the North – my lookout.
And when it comes, spewing

Forth, frothing and teeming
From weatherworn scowls,
Who'll hear our screams
As the winds scour and howl

Above the sound of the choir?
We cower like pups.
Lightning strikes the spire
And burns my arse up.

The Book of Revelation Derby

Place that bet for the race of a lifetime,
Turn out the pockets of your overcoat,
    Dig deep in the sofa.
    Come, my losers, loafers,
Slippery-slopers, leave it all behind,
The unmade beds, unfed pets, unpaid bills,
    Unread written warnings:
    When it's Derby morning
In Heaven, a trail of crisp £10 notes
Leads straight to the door of William Hill.

But why, not even studying the form,
Pick a 66-to-1 outsider,
    A no-hoper, a known
    Fader, a rag-and-bone
Nag? The skies at Epsom build to a storm.
Several horses shy away from the start.
    And then comes the thunder,
    The turf lifting under
Hundreds of hooves: you look for your rider,
See him take the lead with a drumming heart,

His colours flying, sky-blue and maroon.
You fiddle at the buttons of your shirt,
    Already perspiring
    Over signs of tiring
In your filly... Has she gone off too soon?...
When it comes to the death, will she respond?...
    But what compares to this
    Bliss, a lucky-charm kiss,
The roaring crowd, an all-or-nothing spurt,
This end to ploughing the Slough of Despond?

Then at Tattenham Corner, with the others
Closing in fast and five furlongs to go,
        The rain pouring, your poor
        Beast going backwards, four
Wraith-ridden steeds, skeletal stud-brothers,
Scythe through the back-markers, bloodied by whips,
        Scorched by lightning, seething
        At bits, hotly breathing
Down the neck of your knackery-mare, lo!
Outstripping the winds of Apocalypse.

And even now you're shouting yourself hoarse,
Desperate for a last unheard-of burst,
        A second wind to get
        Behind this mulish bet
Of yours; incredibly she feels its force,
Keeps on in terror to the very last.
        The noise diminishes.
        A photo-finish is
Announced, a blurred stampede. You fear the worst
As the stewards enquire into your past.

The Swifts at Cruz Alta

As we gaze on Lisbon through a heat-haze,
Looking down from the Cruz Alta peak,
Hundreds of swifts cut the air to shreds
About the empty cross, about our heads,
A stream of scissoring glissando shrieks.
I always suffer from vertigo these days.

*

Whilst my companion looked for a room
I waited in the middle of Rossío Square
In broad daylight, surrounded by our things
Like a grounded bird with outsize wings.
It was rush hour. Nobody stopped to stare.
I didn't think anything, didn't assume

The worst at his approach, shook my head
Over the hard-luck story, the slab of hash,
But leaned closer as he lowered his voice
And found myself faced with a simple choice
(Poor exchange rate, though he accepted cash):
I have knife. I want money. Else you dead.

*

It seems so small from here. A huge relief,
The city viewed without a single cloud:
All at once the harpy-like swifts
Are working at dizzying speed on a gift
That falls seamlessly from the sky, a shroud,
Covering the sight of a crucified thief.

Closure

Knowing of the closures,
I might not have trusted
my ears from this distance
had it not been for
the twenty-nine crows
(I counted them as souls
as they flew towards me)
that rose raggedly
from the slag-heap
at the sound of a shunt,
a single grating clunk,
from the pit's rusted head.

Hawthorn

The hawthorn blowet swotes
Of everykune tree

We walk the public footpaths, byways
From May to July,
The drovers' roads, the lanes
And bridleways

Hand-in-hand or single-file
Down green aisles,
Crossing tussocky pastures
From stile to stile,

From Applehouse to Crazies Hill –
And all along
The ox-eye daisies gaze,
Songbirds throng,

Grazing sheep and startled deer
Stop and stare
At my *leman*, a sprig of hawthorn
In her hair.

10 July 2004

blowet – blossoms
swotes – sweetest
everykune – every kind
leman – true love